THE ABCs
OF
LIVING
HAPPY

ROGER RAMSEYER

For additional copies visit your
local bookstore or contact:

Rams Roost Press
6346 Eby Road · PO Box 636
Smithville, OH 44677
330-669-2206

ISBN 0-9748611-0-3

First Printing—March 2004
Second Printing—April 2004

Carlisle Printing
OF WALNUT CREEK Ink
2673 Township Road 421
Sugarcreek, OH 44681

CONTENTS

ACKNOWLEDGMENT

Roger Ramseyer is a bright, thoughtful, and insightful educator. He is an outstanding individual.

I have known Roger Ramseyer for over 40 years. In 1979, when he came to Holmes County as the high school principal, I was working as a school administrator, and we became great friends. His ability to achieve great results and yet seemingly balance his life was a model for me.

Roger and I continued to be close associates as he became superintendent of Green Local Schools. Later, when I became the executive director of the Buckeye

Association of School Administrators, we continued to work together at The College of Wooster, where he was a professor.

He is an extremely capable man of high integrity. His leadership and management skills are exemplary. You will enjoy his book, *The ABCs of Living Happy,* as a guide for all of us to balance our lives with living to work or working to live.

Roger Ramseyer receives my highest regards as an educator and as an individual.

> Richard Maxwell
> Executive Director of the Buckeye
> Association of School Administrators
> of Ohio

PRESSING ON —
DETERMINATION

PRESS ON

NOTHING IN THE WORLD CAN TAKE THE PLACE OF PERSISTENCE. TALENT WILL NOT; NOTHING IS MORE COMMON THAN UNSUCCESSFUL MEN WITH TALENT. GENIUS WILL NOT; UNREWARDED GENIUS IS ALMOST A PROVERB. EDUCATION ALONE WILL NOT; THE WORLD IS FULL OF EDUCATED DERELICTS. PERSISTENCE AND DETERMINATION ALONE ARE OMNIPOTENT.

AUTHOR: UNKNOWN

My father taught me the value of hard work. Growing up on a farm, we were expected to be up by 4:30 A.M. and in the barn by 5:00. There were cows to be milked, chickens to be fed, hogs to be slopped, plus much more. At 7:30 it was time to get back to the house for breakfast and get ready for school. Working hard on the farm was not always appreciated, but it certainly taught all family members how to work.

There are many talented people in this world. There are not enough who are really willing to work. Far too many are on the relief rolls who could and should be working.

Do your share to make this a better world. The joy of a job well done is hard to beat. Please give it a try!

EFFECTIVE DISCIPLINE

Prohibitions against bad behavior rarely motivate us to do good. Some even stir up desires to disobey. Tell Johnny to stay away from the cookie jar and soon you'll hear the lid opening. The strongest motivations of good behavior are those in which we have a personal investment.

"A school janitor posted a sign in the front schoolyard that read, 'Please keep off the grass.' But the children continued to run and play in the grass and tromp on the turf.

Then a fourth grade teacher had a neat idea. She decided to have each child in her class plant a crocus bulb in the fall along the edge of the sidewalk. As winter drew to a close, the students eagerly watched for the first signs of spring. Soon the bulbs turned into blooming flowers. What a power those bulbs had to keep dozens of little feet on the right path and off the grass (taken from Dennis DeHaan, *Our Daily Bread*, 1956)."

As teachers, parents, and administrators, we all need to be positive motivators for our children. We need to continually look for positive motivators for our students. It's not easy, but certainly it is a joy when we open the door to successful motivation. Good luck!

FAILURE

How do you react when *you* fail? Maybe you made a nasty comment, or you completed a project, and it didn't go as planned, or a relationship (friendship or marriage) fell apart. How do you handle the next opportunity to make improvements on your past negative record? What do you do?

A kindergarten student failed to color his paper completely and neatly, as per usual. He took the paper home and his mom spoke to him about how important it was to do his homework well. Then, expecting a promise of better things to come, she asked her son, "So what are you going to do about it tomorrow?" He replied, "I'm going to stay home. I'm not going to school!" In other words, rather than facing the problem, he wanted to avoid it!

Now is the time for mom and teacher to step up to the plate. This student needs to be encouraged. It is time to look for the positive in the student's work. You still need to correct and suggest positive improvements but, more importantly, look for something he has done well to reinforce. Now is the time for the adult to really be a teacher. Sometimes, encouragement can be the most important job of the teacher. "When I have failed, I need you to teach this lesson clear: If I but learn and try again, success is always near" (taken from James Branson).

LESSON

WATCH YOUR TONGUE

How many times have you said something that you later regretted? For example, you are having a bad day and so is one of your students. You lose patience and say, "Sit down and shut up," rather than "Will you be quiet, please?" At times you need to be firm—yes, very firm—but always be polite. If you want your student or child to treat you in a polite, respectful manner, and they always should, then you must be an example for them.

The tone of your voice is more

powerful than what you actually say. A quiet, subdued voice may get the job done, but not always. However, a very firm "please" many times will work. Give it a try.

All of us recognize the destructive nature and power of the tongue. Many have warned us about the need to guard our speech.

This bit of verse from an unknown writer says it well: "The boneless tongue, so small and weak, can crush and kill." Also, the Persian proverb wisely says, "A lengthy tongue, an early death." From Hebrews we read, "Though feet should slip, don't let the tongue."

We all lose it, at times, and say something to another that really hurts. When we do, we need to go back to the person we hurt and ask for forgiveness. At times, it may be hard, but it must be done, especially when dealing with children. An approach might be, "Yesterday I lost my temper with you, and I was harsh.....I'm sorry. Please, will you work harder on behaving in class?"

The tongue has been likened to a little fire that sets a great big forest ablaze, or to a small rudder that turns a giant ship in a storm.

In closing, I really like the words of Posegate, as he says:

> THERE ARE SOME SILENT PEOPLE
> WHOSE PRAISE SHOULD BE SUNG;
> THEY PREACH A MIGHTY SERMON
> BY GUARDING WELL THEIR TONGUE.

Give it some thought and be aware of the power of your tongue!

MAKING EYE CONTACT

As a teacher, administrator, or parent it is most important to make eye contact any time you are speaking to another person. There is nothing more distracting than a person who speaks to you and never looks you in the eye. It makes you feel as though you are not really very important, like his thoughts are somewhere else.

If you are disciplining a child, rather than standing at the front of the room and speaking, try walking directly to the person, then look him *directly* in his eye and with a firm, polite voice, ask for cooperation.

Direct eye contact is not easy for many, and you may need to "practice." Find a good friend and sit directly across from one another. As you speak, force yourself to look directly into his eyes and complete your conversation.

I believe you will become a much more effective communicator if you practice making direct eye contact. And, you will get your point across! Good luck!

WHAT I WEAR IS IMPORTANT

It is morning and the alarm goes off. You ask yourself, "What shall I wear today?" This discussion is always important, especially if you are going to be in contact with people. If you are going to spend the day working in the yard or garden, then wear your cutoffs, favorite old shirt, and straw hat—enjoy!

If you are going to be around people, you want to be comfortable and look your best. When you dress in an appropriate manner, you feel more confident and have more energy.

Yes, it is very important to look good on the outside, but it's more important to look good on the inside. We need to clothe ourselves with love, compassion, kindness, humility, patience, and gentleness. As you wear these things, you will find your day goes better. As difficult situations arise, you will handle them in a professional, confident manner.

As Dave Egner said, "How have the days been for you; troubles, bad feelings, anger, hurt? Maybe you need to put on some new clothes?"

Go back up and reread the needed items, just above, and then put them on for the day. Better yet, put them on every day.

Just yesterday, I was having dinner with three of my old college friends, after a round of golf. We were seated and a young lady arrived at our table. She was wearing her *best* clothes. She was friendly, helpful, cheery, and carried a big smile.

This waitress was only 16 years old, but obviously she knew the importance of wearing the right thing, especially on the "inside." Needless to say, she really helped to make our dining experience very enjoyable. When it came time to leave, I carefully noted the tips that were left for her. No one gave her 10%; everyone gave her 20% and more. Her charming, caring personality was rewarded, and yours will be also if you can catch the spirit of wearing your best every day. Well, maybe not every day, but how about 8 out of 10 for a start? You never know, it may become a great habit, and you will be well dressed every day.

You can do it! Give it a try.

LESSON

WORRY — WHY?

Are you a worrywart? Many of us spend far too much time worrying about unimportant things.

A couple took a cruise to Alaska. Even though they really anticipated a great trip, they worried about everything — "Will we have the right clothes? Will the travel be safe? Should we spend the money on the cruise? Will there be medical assistance if we need it?" — and on and on. They finally arrived home and realized they really didn't enjoy the beautiful trip because all they did was worry. Does this sound like you? I hope not, but just in case, let's think about it.

Life is too short to worry it away. Every day is a blessing—enjoy it. Take a walk in the park or in a nearby woods, sit by the lake or ocean and feel the breeze, or call a friend or relative and have a friendly chat. There are so many neat things to do.

Sit down and make a list of "fun things" you'd enjoy doing, and then try to do one every day. If not every day, how about once a week? Many of you work very hard just trying to make ends meet, but it is *very* important to enjoy your days on this earth. Take some time for yourself. Personally, I enjoy working in my vegetable garden and yard. My wife enjoys golfing and working in her flower gardens. What do you enjoy? Please, don't let life pass you by; get to some fun things and stop worrying.

"Don't hurry, don't worry. You're only here for a short visit. So be sure to stop and smell the flowers." Walter C. Hogan has his priorities in order.

According to Amy H. Berger, "It is estimated that more than thirteen million American adults are chronic worriers. The National Institute of Mental Health says anxiety disorders are America's most commonly reported mental health problems."

Worry is not for you—discard it to do something fun today!

GOSSIP

We all know a person who loves to talk about others, and many times in a negative manner. My dad always said, "If you can't say something nice about a person, don't say anything at all." I know his statement was not original, but it was, oh so true. It is just as easy to say something positive about a person as something negative. Then why do we many times catch ourselves speaking negatively?

The first step in correcting this problem is to recognize we are guilty.

Someone said, "When tempted to gossip in a negative manner, breathe through your nose; that's a great way to keep our mouths shut."

There is an antidote to the poison of gossip, and it is love. The Good Book tells us, "You shall love your neighbor as yourself." Whenever we are tempted to speak a negative gossip, how about a word of kindness or respect instead?

It is not unusual for one's reputation to be ruined by just one person. Words of gossip, whether true or false, can do *much* damage to another. So please be aware of what you say, and make it a point to say something positive about a friend or neighbor every day. Remember, if you can't say something nice about a person, don't say it. Maybe someone will say something nice about you in return. Have a great day!

CRITICISM

Criticism is part of life. Having served as a school superintendent, I know that people will criticize many decisions you make. We all must learn to let negative comments run off our back, just like water runs off the back of a duck.

Today, we have a shortage of school superintendents and principals, many times because those who are qualified do not want to hear constant criticism.

As I read several newspapers daily, I am amazed at the amount of criticism our U.S. President must endure. To be a leader is *not* easy and you must be willing to accept criticism. However, as a loving people, we must be very careful to be fair-minded. As we criticize, we must also look for the good and comment to the positive when appropriate.

It was always a great day when I received a note from a student, parent, or board member that read, "Thanks" for doing something correctly. If you know someone in a position of leadership and they have a success or do something well, pick up the phone or write a note and let them know. We need good leaders, and we can only keep them if they know they are appreciated, at least part of the time.

Be sure your criticism is fair! By living in the United States, we do have freedom of speech and it is wonderful. However, be a positive person and don't be *too* critical.

It matters not what others say
In ridicule or fun;
I want to live that I may hear
Him say to me, well done!

      — Beers

ATTITUDE

As we work with children and adults, a positive attitude is very, very important. Confidence is developed by the attitudes and practices of the people who influence our lives, such as parents, teachers, and administrators. Without confidence, it is very difficult to be a success. Do you send positive messages each day? Have you said the following to your child or student: "You're always making a mess," "You are such a baby," "Why are you always screwing up?"

"Can't you do anything right?" "Why are you always last?"

Hearing negative comments, like those above, can only cause a child or adult to react in a negative manner. You can build confidence by saying one of the following: "You really look nice today." "You did a great job on that project." "I like your style; you are going to be a real success." By verbally demonstrating faith in one's efforts, you are well on your way to building positive attitudes. For years I've been a real fan of Norman Vincent Peale. If you haven't read his book, *The Power of Positive Thinking,* please do so. One of my favorite quotes from his book is: "It's your attitude, not your aptitude, that determines your altitude." Melinda Hill, our extension agent, suggests the following:

1. Have a positive attitude; be direct, descriptive, and nonjudgmental.

2. Be aware of your body language; maintain eye contact; and be careful to control the tone of your voice and the timing of your message.
3. Begin discussions positively whenever possible. Don't come out fighting!
4. Try to get agreement on minor points, leading up to major points.
5. Always respect the other person's time. Be on time *always,* or call ahead and change the meeting time.
6. Have confidence that you can deal with the situation and all will come out winners.

The above suggestions are all positive and will help you to a positive outcome in a conference or evaluation. Again, being positive and confident will make your day.

There are many listings for parents and teachers to help with a positive attitude. I would suggest a few for your consideration: Express genuine compliments, think positive thoughts, be courteous, support children's events by being there, practice constructive criticism, work together, and remember it is okay to make a mistake.

Charles Swindoll is another great writer on having a positive attitude. He says, "Attitude is more important than facts. It is more important than education, than money…, than failures, than successes, than appearance…, than giftedness or skill….I am convinced that life is 10% what happens to me and 90% of how I react to it. And so it is with you—we are in charge of our attitudes."

Now, it is time for you to look at your own attitude. Do you want to improve your present attitude? In life, it is not possible to be 100% positive 100% of the time. However, you can laugh more, pay compliments to your children and friends, send a card or flowers to those you love, plus much more.

Everyone enjoys being around a person with a good attitude. Do others want to be around you? Please, work on a positive attitude for a happier life, and we will all want to be around you more.

"Please" and "Thank You"

It is so pleasing to be around people with good manners, especially young people. In order to enjoy this pleasure, we, as adults, must teach politeness.

During my high school principal days, I would try to talk to my teaching staff on a regular basis concerning different areas of responsibility. At one faculty meeting, I spoke to the teachers about "being an example—practicing good manners in the classroom by using 'please' and 'thank you' on a regular basis." Much to my pleasure, two teachers stopped in my office a couple of months later and explained how they had taken my suggestion of using "please" and "thank you" in their home economics classes. Much to their surprise, their students soon began to do the same as they spoke during class time. They were so excited about their examples being accepted as proper behavior by their students.

We as parents or teachers cannot expect young people to be polite unless we are positive examples. It is just as easy to say, "Will you please take a seat," as it is to say, "Sit down." Or, "Thank you for all your good help today," rather than saying nothing at all. "Please" and "thank you" are small words that can make our big world a more fun place to reside.

Please, give it a try, and I think you'll find joy in the results.

LESSON *L*

BE ALL YOU CAN BE

We have been given so much! Many of our abilities remain hidden for years, and suddenly, for some of us, they appear. Not everyone is so lucky, but I firmly believe that only you yourself can make positive things happen.

Your parents and teachers can encourage and teach you, but only you can determine the *someone* you really want to be.

The alcoholic can never be cured until he decides it is time and he really wants to make a change. Our lives are the same—we won't change until we really want to be a good person who lives life to the fullest.

Ralph Manston, in the following poem, really hits the nail on the head—read and enjoy:

Be someone who listens, and you will be heard. Be someone who cares, and you will be loved. Be someone who gives, and you will be blessed. Be someone who comforts, and you will know peace.

Be someone who genuinely seeks to understand, and you will be wise. Be someone kind, someone considerate, and you will be admired. Be someone who values truth, and you will be respected. Be someone who takes action, and you will move life forward.

Be someone who lifts others higher, and your life will be rich. Be someone

filled with gratitude, and there will be
no end to the things for which you'll be
thankful.

Be someone who lives with joy, with
purpose, as your own light brightly shines.
Be, in every moment, the special someone
you are truly meant to be.

LESSON

SMELL THE ROSES

We are so busy! Never taking time to really enjoy all we have. At least, this is the case with many of us.

In our world, life is fast-paced and busy. Many jobs require 50-80 hours a week, plus for working mothers, many more hours at home caring for the family.

Back in 1992, I sat down and wrote, "There is Still Time." Maybe it will be helpful for you to read it. Maybe you want to write your own "There is Still Time"?

If I could live my life again, I would

smell the roses. I would take more time away from work to appreciate natural beauty around me — the birds, the trees, the flowers, the green grass, the meandering streams, and yes, the bugs and weeds.

I would walk barefoot in the sand and let the warm, bright rays of sun wash my face with dripping sweat.

I would spend more time with family and friends, appreciating their skills, listening to their problems and concerns, and enjoying their sense of humor.

I would spend more time "working" in my gardens, getting dirty hands, grit under my fingernails, sore knees, and aching muscles. I would watch more carefully my God at work, growing the vegetables and flowers. I would eat more fresh fruit and vegetables from my own yard and garden.

I would spend more time dangling worms in the local pond and enjoy more fresh fish on the supper table. I would worry less about a clean house, orderly workshop, and tidy barn. Instead, I would walk the grassy fields, the quiet woodlands, and the roadsides, enjoying nature around me.

Wait a minute, my life is not over! I can still do it. I'll start today!

DEALING WITH "BULLIES"

As a parent, many of you have had to deal with a bully, just to protect your child. The bully causes a lot more difficulty than many of us realize.

Having served as a school principal for many years, I have dealt with many bullies. Some were verbally abusive, but many were physically abusive. You cannot allow a bully to continue negative actions in a public school setting. There are many students who are afraid to go to school! You ask, "How can this happen and why doesn't the teacher or principal do something about it?"

First, many times the teacher does not know the extreme negative effect the bully is having on another student. Unless the affected student tells his or her teacher or parent, the student may never get the help he or she needs. Be sure you talk to your kids, and encourage them to let you know if they are being bullied. They need to know that it's not okay to be hit, spit upon, cursed, or have their lunch money taken by force. This happens over and over every day.

What do I think should happen to this above-described bully? I think he needs to be bent over and paddled. Yes, I am from the old school, and I believe in paddling. Paddling needs to be done with another person present as a witness, and only after the parent or guardian has been notified. I have paddled many students, and only one time did I have a problem. Always, I explained to the student why he was being punished and gave him or her a chance to question my decision. Yes, I paddled both boys and girls.

The one time I had a problem, the mother called Children Services and complained that I had been "too severe on her child." He had beaten up at least eight students before he was paddled. The guidance counselor came to me, as superintendent of the schools, and asked, "What can I do?" We called the student in and explained to him, in no uncertain terms, that his behavior would no longer be tolerated. The building principal, in the building this student attended, did not believe in corporal punishment as it was against his philosophy. Now, I ask you, is it okay for innocent students to get beaten up for no good reason? I think not! After he was paddled, he did not beat up another student. He had gotten to the point in his behavior that he was about to be expelled from school. Was it better to paddle him and keep him in school, or would it have been better to have him on the street out of school beating up someone? Children Services spent three days in our school district investigating my actions and paddling. After speaking with many parents, teachers, and students, they decided the paddling was justified.

Now you know why many principals and superintendents will no longer paddle. Long investigations and expensive lawsuits quickly discourage the administrator from doing his job. I always said, "If they are going to put me in jail, then let it be for my doing my job and running a tight school district."

As an administrator, you don't have to paddle often if the students know it is an option. We did a telephone survey in my district and 91% of the parents indicated they wanted to keep corporal punishment as an option, 6% had no opinion, and 3% said they did not want their child paddled. I took this report to my Board of Education, and at the last board meeting before I retired, the District Board adopted a policy making corporal punishment an option for the administration. In our county, we are the only school district that still permits the paddle to be used, and it is not used often.

In 1993, a parent from Ohio wrote in the local paper, "My son, Aaron, was assaulted by a classmate last week…it was not an isolated incident. The boy, with the help of some of his friends, had beaten up my son before….I do not know what to do….I don't know what to tell my son, and I don't know why kids act that way. I told him to tell his teachers. His response, "They don't care, Mom. They just say, 'Knock it off, boys.'"…My son is scared and is afraid to go to school. I called the principal and asked what the #@!? was going on and why wasn't he controlling that school? "It's not a perfect world and things happen," he replied. Yes, things happen because teachers and administrators allow them to happen… why is this boy not being punished?… The lack of discipline tells children that deviant behavior is all right, and they continue doing it! These bullies have taken something very precious from my son—his dignity. My son even thinks he deserves this brutal treatment. Why not? It's happened so often and nothing is being done….During the day my mind is not on my job. I'm too busy thinking about a little boy, whom I dearly love, and I wonder if he's safe at school."

In my opinion, those teachers and principal are totally at fault. If you cannot control your school, then you need to look for another job. This parent needs to take this problem to the local police and file charges. She probably doesn't want to take this step, but her most prized possession, her son, needs her help immediately! Never permit a teacher or principal to step away from his responsibility to protect your child.

Too many parents of the bully will not admit their child is wrong. "My little Johnny or Jane would never hurt another child," they say. Don't bet on it and look very carefully at the behavior patterns of your children. Step up to the plate and be a responsible parent, rather than make excuses. "I'm a single parent," "I'm unemployed," "Let the school handle it," "I didn't have custody when it happened," etc., etc.

As reported in the *Akron Beacon Journal* on December 17, 1993, on page A5, "more than one teacher in 10 and one student in four have been victims in or near their public schools in the past year…." In all, the report detailed a culture of violence and intimidation that is stumping many educators.

Schools need to tighten up, and Boards of Education need to hire principals and superintendents who are not afraid to do their jobs. Yes, the courts need to be challenged and parents need to support good principals. They are not easy to find these days.

The message needs to get out that bullies are in for a tough day!

MONEY AND MONEY MANAGEMENT

Why do we even talk about money? Because without it, life can be difficult; and by not knowing how to manage money, extra unnecessary stress is a real possibility.

Many of our children today know nothing about money because it has always been there for them, and they never needed to learn money management. What an eye-opener when they get out on their own!

During my high school principal days, I realized that many students had no training regarding money. They did not even know how to balance a checkbook or make change from a $20 bill without using a computer. Computers can be used to assist one's daily living, but many could not survive without a calculator or computer. Many students do not know basic math facts, as they have been taught to rely on mechanics to do the work for them.

In one school where I was principal, we put a course in the business department called, "Basic Math for Daily Living." Not a large percentage of the students had a chance to take the course because of the rigid demands of the college curriculum, and they felt they just didn't have time for the course. However, in final evaluation, those who took the money course ranked it near the top as their favorite, most useful course. They not only learned to balance a checkbook, but also learned investing, interest rates, buying a home, buying and selling stocks and bonds, and, most importantly, balancing a budget. Several students who were college bound ranked the course #1 when asked, "What courses were most valuable during your high school days?"

As parents and teachers, we must remember the importance of teaching math and money management. My wife taught sixth grade in a public school where many Amish students attended. The parents of the Amish children wanted their children to learn math, reading, and writing and to forget all the other "frills." Maybe they are right; maybe we try to put too much "other stuff" into the curriculum? Believe me, those Amish kids knew their math facts, as their parents insisted that it is important.

As William Somerset Maugham said, "There is nothing as degrading as the constant anxiety about one's means of livelihood. Money is like a sixth sense without which you cannot make a complete use of the other five."

Many people make a lot of money during a lifetime, and when it comes time to retire, they have very little. Why? Because they have either wasted it, or not managed it well. My dad always told me, "When you earn a dollar, give 10 cents to the church and save 10 cents for a rainy day." I've pretty much followed his advice; however, Uncle Sam seems to be getting more than his share at times. It is not how much you make, but how much you save. How many times have you heard this wise old saying? Too many of us do not listen to this old adage and live only for today. What a mistake! We must teach our children to save and invest wisely. It is not easy to save without help from a wise parent or teacher.

Usually in a marriage one person is the better money manager. My wife is very conservative and watches every penny, and that is not bad. I, on the other hand, am a risk taker and, at times, make bad investments. In other words, I need to slow down and do more research before plunking down my hard-earned dollars in an investment. My wife will get on the computer and research before making an investment, whereas I am more likely to jump into a stock I heard the boys raving about at the coffee shop. In this case, I believe my wife has the better plan.

When going to buy an item, I never pay the "asking price." I like to haggle. You would be amazed at how much you can save by not paying the asking price. Recently, I wanted to buy a new pick-up truck. The initial price I was quoted was $22,990 and three days later I bought the truck for $17,000. Now that is quite a savings. If you go to buy a major item and pay the initial asking price, I venture to guess you are spending way too much. Don't be in a hurry to buy and know the value before you go shopping. In case you are buying a car or truck, be very careful about "extras."

Money is not all-important, and it should not control your life. But it is important enough to not waste your hard-earned dollars. Good luck!

By the way, remember you must teach your own children money management. Do not wait until they go off to college and run up a $10,000 credit bill!

BE CAREFUL TO JUDGE

Many of us were taught at a young age to not judge another but rather to look at ourselves and judge only ourselves. As it says in Matthew 7:5, "First remove the plank from your own eye, and then you'll see clearly."

By judging others, we many times appear arrogant, especially if we discuss our judgments in open forum or even with friends.

We do need to make judgments pertaining to right and wrong. Otherwise, we would agree with anything and everything others do. Using bad language, stealing, and fighting are wrong and making a judgment not to do those actions is a good thing.

Many of us turn to our religion for discussions on right or wrong, and again, I think this is good as long as the church stays strong and doesn't compromise its principles. Some believe the church has become lax recently and has not upheld the high principles we once expected. I hope this is not the case in your church. Hopefully, right is still right and wrong is still wrong.

I once had a guidance counselor working for me, in a school where I served as principal, who judged much too quickly. Yes, I know, there I go judging him, but let me finish. He once told a young man that "he was not college material…and he should not go on to college but, rather, get a job and go to work right out of high school." This student was very offended and came and told me about it. He was very distressed and upset that he had been judged as "incompetent" by his guidance counselor. He went on to college, graduated, got a good job in sales, and came back to remind the counselor that "he made far more money than the counselor would ever dream of making."

In this case, the judgment worked out fine as it pushed the student to prove he could do it, and he did. However, not all students would react in this manner. Most would probably listen to the wise old counselor and not go to college. So be careful how you judge, especially your own children. Many can do more than you ever thought possible if you encourage them in a positive manner.

Remember, "Judge not or ye may be judged!"

GIVE MORE, SPEND LESS

There are many needy people out there whom you can really help. What do you have to give? Some of you have money, others talent, or maybe just some time that could be spent with a friendly visit.

Many people are not able to get out and about, as they are physically unable to drive a car or even work. A cheerful visit is worth more to this person than a $100 bill.

A member in our church had a stroke and is confined to his bed in a rest home. I try to visit him at least twice a month. He so enjoys those minutes I spend with him because it gives him a chance to catch up on the "outside news" as he calls it. He is always so very appreciative of my 15 to 20-minute visits that I almost feel guilty for not staying longer or visiting more often. I really do enjoy my visits, and it makes me feel like I am doing something right. Try it, and I believe you'll think of your time as well spent. We are all busy, but an hour a month spent visiting a homebound person is time well spent.

If you are fortunate and have more money than you really need, why not share some of it with a needy friend? We all know people who have far less than we do. Our first responsibility is to take care of oneself and our family. After this has been accomplished, maybe we should look for a worthy cause and give some of our "extra" to help another? Yes, I know, every day you get a request in the mail for "help;" but look for a good charity and try giving some money or time, and I assure you, it will make you feel good and it will be appreciated.

We all need to spend less and give more. It has taken me a lifetime to realize I don't need all that "stuff." My wife complains about having to clean around all the collectibles I've brought home, and she is right. We just plain don't need it all, and slowly I am getting rid of much, and not bringing home more.

Deciding to spend less is a personal choice, or it could be a family choice. How many of you spend far too much at Christmas? How about buying one gift instead of five or six for one person? Again, does anyone really need all that "stuff?" You can then take the extra money you save and buy something for another child or adult who has nothing. Sounds pretty simple, doesn't it? However, how many of us put it into practice? I know several who have tried the one-gift-only approach, and they are just as happy as they were with five or six. If relationships are high on your list of priorities, then maybe you will want to give more by giving some away.

Lastly, be careful to whom and where you give, as there are a lot of freeloaders and "lazys" out there. Pick your recipients carefully and enjoy the good feeling of helping another in need.

THE VALUE OF WORK

Having been born and raised on a farm, I was expected to work! Not 8 hours a day, but until the work was finished—many times, 15 hours in a day. At 4 A.M. we were up and out in the barn, ready to milk the cows, feed the heifers, slop the pigs, and gather the eggs. Getting up in the morning was not an option; it was a "duty call."

At the time, when I was growing up, I did not always appreciate getting up at 4 A.M. to help with the farm chores, but now I appreciate it a lot. As a matter of fact, it is now 4:10 in the morning, and I'm on my second cup of coffee, writing this lesson. Mornings are great, and my brain works best early in the morning. By 5 a.m. the roosters will be crowing, calling me to the barn for their grain and water. By noon, I'll have 8 hours of work completed already and still have all those hours remaining in the afternoon. After a noon lunch, a 30-minute "catnap" refreshes me, and I'm ready to go.

I don't know who said it, but the saying: "Early to bed, early to rise, makes a man healthy, wealthy, and wise," is a great one. I really love the mornings, and to sit on my deck and watch the sun come up is just about heaven.

There is a lot more to life than work. Family comes to mind immediately. However, on the farm, you were up working *with* family and everyone was pitching in to make life easier. My brother had his chores, and each of my sisters was expected to "carry their load" as well.

In our church bulletin one Sunday in 1990 I read the following and clipped it out for future reference:

"Which are you?" someone said, "there are four kinds of "bones" in every organization. There are the *wishbones* who spend their time wishing someone else would do the work. There are the *jawbones* who do all the talking but very little else. Next there are the *knucklebones* who knock everything anyone ever tries to do. Finally, there are the *backbones* who get under the load and do the work."

I hope you are the *backbones* and shoulder your share of the load! Work is not something to be dreaded, but rather a wonderful gift each of us has the opportunity to do, unless, of course, a handicap keeps us away from work. Find something you enjoy doing, and then put yourself into the job. Certainly family and friends are still important and need your time also, but completing a job and doing it well can be a source of real joy and fulfillment. As David McCasland said, "No matter what our occupation, we must keep our work in perspective; God and family are more important than dedication to a job. Work is a gift, not a god."

I agree, these two things mentioned, "family and God," are more important, but work is a close third.

Get up early and enjoy your job today!

LESSON

SMILE AND SAY, "HELLO"

Are you a friendly person? This is an area I need to work on daily. Maybe you need help in this area also? Some people have many friends and others don't seem to have any. Why?

If you want to have friends, you *must* learn to go out to people. You cannot sit back and wait for people to come to you; rather, you must speak up with a big smile and friendly, "Hello," and strike up a conversation. Other people are looking for friendships also, and your friendly "Hello" may be the needed opening to a long-term relationship.

Daily, I go to the local post office to pick up my mail. I always run into the same people and often stop to chat. I noticed one man coming in daily, always with a smug face and never looking up or speaking. I decided to smile and say, "Hello." After several attempts at being friendly, he finally started saying, "Good morning." Now, he not only says, "Good morning," but many times he stops to talk. I truly believe his day is happier because he stops to chat. He recently lost his wife to an unexpected heart attack, and life was probably not a lot of fun for him. Slowly he is coming back; going to church, working out at the YMCA, and putting out a garden.

We all have difficult times in our lives and maybe a friendly smile and "Hello" will start our engine again. I hope so, because we all need a friend!

LISTEN MORE, SPEAK LESS

"A WISE OLD BIRD SAT ON AN OAK—
THE MORE HE SAW, THE LESS HE SPOKE,
THE LESS HE SPOKE, THE MORE HE HEARD;
LORD, MAKE ME LIKE THAT WISE OLD BIRD."
—ANONYMOUS

Many of us talk too much. We all know others who talk continually. It is not only annoying, but normally no one listens to the "babbler." It has been estimated that a very talkative person speaks up to 30,000 words a day! Now that's way too much!

Our children learn from us, and if we are constantly babbling, then probably our kids will do the same. We need to set a good example. I remember my dad saying, "Speak when spoken to." Maybe I spoke too often, growing up, and this was his way of reminding me to slow down and not talk so much.

I was talking to a college professor and asked, "Do you remember my brother, as he was in your class in the 60s?" He replied, "I sure do. He was the one who rarely spoke in class, but when he did, everyone sat up and listened." My brother is gone, but what a wonderful way to remember him. His words were few, but when he spoke, it was time to "listen up."

A good teacher or professor gives his students time to speak. Many of my successful classes have been those where I threw out a question and sat back and listened to the students debate the answers. In other words, I was listening and others were talking, even though I was directing the class. I would encourage all of you in education to give plenty of time for your students to respond to your thoughts and questions. There are a lot of bright students out there and they have much to offer. It is our job to draw them out, and then point out the "super comments" to the other members in the class.

To listen is to learn!

L E S S O N

THE IMPORTANCE OF
WRITING A NOTE

Do you enjoy receiving a personal note from a friend? I do, and I also enjoy sending notes.

If you go to the mailbox and receive a happy note, it will usually make your day. So why not make someone else's day by sending a cheerful note?

In our busy world, it is easy to forget to send a "thank you" for the nice birthday gift you received from Grandma. But please remember, Grandma is alone, and she loves to hear from you, if not a written note, at least a phone call.

Too many times I hear, especially older people say, "I wonder if Johnny got my gift; I never heard from him." This is unforgivable! If someone takes the time to send you a gift, it is most definitely your responsibility to respond. As parents, we must teach our children this very important lesson. Also, the teacher can incorporate this in her everyday lesson as well.

During the holidays, many students give gifts to their teacher, especially in elementary school. Each child who gives a gift should receive a "thank you" from the teacher, in writing. Teachers are very busy people, but this is an important lesson to give your students. Please take time to write the note. Parents also enjoy getting notes from the teacher, especially one telling them their child did something well. Notes coming home from the teacher need to be positive, at times, rather than always a note complaining about work not done or bad behavior. Try to balance it out, if you are teaching.

Also, if someone does something nice for you, drop that person a note. We all enjoy knowing that we are appreciated, especially if we go out of our way to do something nice for another. A thoughtful person is an appreciated person.

Do you send a note when a friend or acquaintance has a death in the family? Again, in my opinion, this is an important time to let someone know that you do care and are thinking about him or her. It does not have to be a relative only, but you may send a note to a neighbor, church member, or lodge member, plus others.

Do you keep notes you receive from people? I do. To me, a personal note is something to pick up and reread. I enjoy receiving a personal note; therefore, I better remember to send one when the opportunity arises.

TO FORGIVE

All of us have been wronged
somewhere along life's trail. Life is
not always fair, and at times we receive
the raw end of the deal, many times
undeserved.

Fortunately, I am the type of person
who does not hold a grudge. All of us are
different, and for some, it is hard to forget
and move on. This is something we all
need to work on continually. Certainly it
is not healthy to hold a grudge. Let it roll
off your back like water off a duck's back.

If someone wrongs you and you cannot

let it drop, I suggest you confront the
person, face-to-face, and try to work out
your differences. Many times you'll get an
apology, and at other times, you'll realize
you possibly misunderstood, and it wasn't
meant to hurt you. In a few instances,
the face-to-face meeting will accomplish
nothing. In that scenario, it is up to you to
drop it and move on. As my mom used to
say, "Life is too short to carry negatives
on your shoulder."

Years ago I lent a "friend" some money
when he told me, "My wife has cancer,
and I need the money to pay doctor bills."
It later came to light that he was a heavy
gambler and had lost a lot of money at the
track. His wife was not ill, and, in reality,
he was "borrowing" money from many
people. By the time he was found out, he
had "borrowed" well over $150,000 and
all was lost. It was hard for me to forgive
and forget, especially since my wife had

warned me not to give him the money,
as we were just starting out and did not
have the money to lose. We lost it, and
I learned a valuable lesson about money
management. It was an expensive lesson,
but one that helped me the rest of my
life — be very careful how you invest your
hard-earned money, and maybe listen to
your wife more often. By the way, I do
not hold a grudge against this person, but
rather took it as a valuable lesson and
moved on.

Learn to forgive and you'll be a much
happier person. It is not always easy!

LESSON

JUDGE NOT

How many times have you made a judgment concerning a person, even before you meet him or her, based upon what someone else has told you? I would guess your answer is the same as mine, far too many.

Early on in my career, I was about to take a new job, and I was told by others that I would not like my new boss...as he was hard to get along with and very demanding.

Thankfully, I went into the job with an open mind and a desire to get along with and respect my new boss. As I worked with him, I found him to be very hardworking and, yes, demanding, but also very appreciative when I did a good job. At the time, I was teaching and working in high school. He was my principal and always present at our games, congratulating our team when they won and encouraging us to do even better. Many notes were received from my principal encouraging me to do even better and congratulating us on a recent victory. His encouragement, in my opinion, had a lot to do with our team winning the state championship.

My boss had high expectations and continually expected us to win and perform at a very high level, but without his encouragement, would we have won?

He was one of the best bosses I ever had, and until the day he died, we continued to be great friends. If I had listened to others before I took that job, I may never have had the opportunity to work with this winner. Also, I would have missed out knowing a wonderful person and friend.

The moral of the story is to not listen to others when it comes to judging another; but rather, get to know the person yourself and enter the relationship with an open, positive mind, and you just might make a new friend!

The Good Book says it best in Luke 6:37, "Do not judge, and you will not be judged; do not condemn, and you will not be condemned. Forgive, and you will be forgiven." The forgive part we have not talked about, but we'll save that for another lesson.

Remember, go into a new relationship with an open mind, and you may make a great friend.

LESSON X

BORED — WHY?

There are many who complain that life is boring, and there is nothing exciting to do, especially older folks who are retired.

Nothing could be further from the truth. There are many things you can do when you get the bored feeling. I will list just a few:

1. Go to the library and get a good book. Find your area of interest and sit down and enjoy.

2. Volunteer your time at your local hospital or food pantry. Not only will you be filling a much-needed slot, but you will also feel good about yourself because you are helping a great cause.

3. Visit a person who is homebound or a friend in the hospital.

4. Take a walk in the woods, along the lake or ocean, or just in your back yard. Take notice of all the natural beauty around you, both plants and animals plus the grasses and sky. Nature is really a wonderful gift to each of us.

5. Visit a relative, especially one who lives alone. Maybe someone you've not seen for some time.

6. Join a club that might interest you, i.e. flower club, wine tasting,

investment, homemaker, or as my wife did, a Bev's Club—a group of women from many different backgrounds who all have the first name "Bev."

7. Volunteer as a teacher's aide at your local school. There are always students who could learn from you. Call the principal and volunteer your services.

8. Go to the YMCA or YWCA and work out.

9. Find the place in your local community where people meet for coffee in the morning and stop for a friendly chat.

10. Thank your maker for the many blessings you've received and read a morning devotion.

I could list many more. Hopefully, you'll find something in the above list that will help relieve your boredom if, indeed, you are bored.

Remember, life is a gift. Please try to enjoy each day.

If you are indeed severely bored or depressed, see your doctor and ask for help. The medical profession can work miracles if you really need help.

DECISIONS

Many people really have difficulty when it comes to making a decision. Part of growing up and becoming a mature parent is learning to make decisions.

Too many people want to make a decision by "committee." I once had a boss who could not make a decision. He would never give a "yes" or "no" answer, and I hated it. I really wasn't that concerned about what his decision might be, but rather that he make a decision one way or another. He was constantly creating a committee to discuss the situation and make a decision. Not good!

I want a boss who weighs the issues carefully and thoughtfully, makes a decision, and then lives with it.

It is impossible to always make the right decision, but a good leader will, most times, be successful in decision-making. As a parent, you better be able to make a decision and stick by it. If not, your children will never know your expectations and their parameters. When you make a decision that Johnny needs to be home by 12 midnight, be sure he knows you really mean it, and he is, indeed, expected home by 12, not 12:30.

Decision-making is easy for a few and difficult for many. If it is difficult for you, first accept that fact and work very hard to make decisions. Set a time line for coming up with a firm answer and then *stick* with it.

You will be much more respected if you are a decision-maker, even if you make a mistake once in a while; rather than a fence-sitter who never quite gets it done.

Harry S. Truman said, "Once a decision was made, I did not worry about it afterward."

President Truman did not second-guess himself; he made a decision and lived with it. Maybe more of us need to follow his example.

YOUR HEALTH

Good health and happiness many times go hand-in-hand. Many who do not have good health are happy, but it is a lot easier if you take care of yourself and maintain a healthy lifestyle.

There are many things you can do to maintain your health, and the first that comes to mind is getting your annual physical exam, especially those of us who are over 50 years of age. If we do have a problem, it is much easier to treat if it is found early. We have wonderful doctors who can really work miracles if we only give them a chance. Stay healthy so you can stay around for your loved ones.

In our daily lives we are asked to do many things. Learn to say "No" if you already have enough on your plate. We all need to do our share, but don't get bogged down with too many assignments. There is always someone else who can serve on a committee, if you already are serving on many. As a coworker of mine once told me, "…busy days and months and years without sometimes placing yourself first is harmful—martyrdom can be lethal—take time to be alone with one's self, ideas, and thoughts."

How many times have you cut your sleep time short? I know, I do it all of the time. Rest is very important to the body. My doctor indicates that everyone should get eight hours of sleep a night and some need even more.

Eating correctly is also very important.

Do you eat breakfast or do you just grab a cup of coffee? I see many students on the college campus drinking a Coke for breakfast. Breakfast is a very important meal that none of us should skip. Also, fruits and veggies are great for good health. I recently read in a health magazine that "we all should have five servings of fruit daily" along with lots of fish and chicken. Beef is great, but don't overdo it. Do you drink milk? Healthy bones are needed, and drinking three glasses of milk daily certainly is a plus. Many have osteoporosis as they age, and eating smart certainly is a positive.

I've saved my most important point for last and that is *exercise.* Walking is wonderful and we should all find at least 30 minutes a day to exercise. Some of you swim, bicycle, jazzercise, jog etc.—all are great. However, many do nothing. If you are one who does nothing, start by walking, even if it is only a short distance. Don't make excuses for not walking, just put it on your calendar as "your time." If you don't learn to care for yourself, who will do it? We are ultimately all responsible for ourselves and we need to live life to its fullest by "working" to stay healthy. Thirty minutes a day certainly would be a great beginning. Will you do it?

ABOUT THE AUTHOR

The author of this book was born and raised on a farm in rural Ohio. He attended The College of Wooster, and after graduation, moved to Cleveland, Ohio, where he was a teacher, coach, and high school principal. He then moved to Holmes County where he was the high school principal. From Holmes County he moved to the same farm where he was born. He also served as principal and superintendent of schools in the same district he attended as a youngster growing up in Smithville, Ohio. He retired from public education in 1993.

Currently, Roger Ramseyer serves on

the faculty at The College of Wooster as an adjunct professor. He has been in this position at the College for eleven years.

His wife, Beverly, is a retired elementary school teacher of 30 years, and daughter, Becky, is a practicing attorney in Columbus, Ohio.

As he has said many times, "Life is good."

THE RAMSEYER FAMILY. ROG. BECKY. AND BEV (LEFT TO RIGHT).